BETTER
Homes and
Marriages

249/GI

O. J. Gibson

Christian Family Life

Produced as a service to the Lord's people by Fairhaven Ministries,
an outreach of Fairhaven Bible Chapel, 401 MacArthur Boulevard, San Leandro,
California. Fairhaven is an independent, autonomous, New Testament church
dedicated to evangelism and discipleship through the matrix of local churches
(Matthew 28:19-20; Acts 2:42).

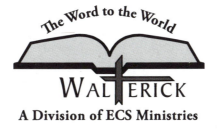

The Word to the World

WALTERICK

A Division of ECS Ministries

Better Homes and Marriages

O. J. Gibson

Published by:

Walterick

(A division of ECS Ministries)

P.O. Box 1028

Dubuque, IA 52004-1028

phone: (563) 585-2070

email: ecsorders@ecsministries.org

website: www.ecsministries.org

First Printed 1994

Reprinted 2009

ISBN 978-1-59387-110-9

Printed in the United States of America

How to Get the Most Out of Your Study

The following suggestions will help make this study more profitable.

Please note that the material is printed with a wide margin to enable you to make notes alongside the text as you study. Space has also been provided to write your answers in the Discussion Questions section of each lesson. The questions are designed to reinforce the lesson material and help you apply the truths in your life.

There are three approaches to studying; Personal, On-on-One, and in a Class Setting.

Before You Start Your Study

In each of these approaches, before you start ask God to help you understand His Word. Claim the promise of Psalm 119:130: "The entrance of Your Words gives light; it gives understanding to the simple." (NKJV) It is impossible to truly understand God's Word without God's help (1 Corinthians 2:14).

Reading the Lesson Material

This part applies for each of the approaches

Read the Notes

Read and reread the lesson. Underline key thoughts, mark anything that you do not understand or that you have questions about. Make notations in the wide margin at the side of each lesson.

Look Up Key References

As time permits, read all Scripture references from a modern translation such as the New American Standard Bible. A typical reference is written with the name of the book followed by the chapter number and verse number which are separated by a colon (example: Colossians 3:23). The abbreviation "cf." means to compare two references (example: Psalm 45:6-7, cf. Hebrews 1:8). Most Bibles have a table of contents that lists the starting page number for each book of the Bible. After finding the page, locate the appropriate chapter and verse.

Answer Discussion Questions

Complete all items in the text and Discussion questions as directed. If you have trouble with a question pass on to the next one.

Personal Study

After completing each lesson, mediate and pray about what you have learned. Ask God to help you apply the truths to your life. Keep the notes for future reference and to share with others.

One-on-One Study

Select a partner for the study. After each of you completes the lesson (see Reading the Lesson Material above) meet to discuss your answers and then prayer together and help each other be accountable for applying the lessons in your lives.

Class Study

Complete "Reading the Lesson Material" (see above)

Attend Class Regularly

There will be a time for small group interaction as well as a lecture period. Your questions ands comments will encourage others to share.

Save Your Notes and Material

These will help you in your further study and you may wish to share them with others.

Table of *Contents*

Section/Title	Page

One Flesh
or Two Individuals

The title of this course is suggested by a well-known magazine, *Better Homes and Gardens*. In a sense, marriage and family are like a garden. It needs much care and hard work to keep it maintained and blooming properly. People who plant or trim in their yards and gardens and use enriching compounds can be expected to have the best results. So it is with marriage. Those who have as a major objective the cultivation of a healthy, happy marriage and family life, and *work diligently* to make it so, will have the best results.

Good results come when we pay attention to expert counsel. In the case of human beings, created by God in His image and for His pleasure, that expert is the Creator Himself. His "manufacturer's manual" is the Bible, literally, "The Book." Marriage was instituted by God immediately after the beginning of creation for the benefit of the creatures. He said, "It is not good for man to be alone. I will make him a helpmeet suitable for him" (Gen. 2:18). This does not mean that a single life cannot be successful. It means that a man is made a social being for companionship and fellowship. A primary way to fulfill this need is in marriage, although it can come in other ways. In particular, God made man to live as two sexes, male and female. He could have done it another way, as He demonstrated in other species.

God joined man and woman in marriage as "one flesh" (Gen. 2:24), an expression much more profound than people seem to realize. The Lord Jesus picked up this expression in His remarks about the enduring quality of marriage according to the intention of God (Matt. 19:4-6). Furthermore, marriage is used as an illustration and model, intended by God to be an object lesson of the relationship between the Lord Jesus Christ and His people, the Church (Eph. 5:31-32).

Husband and wife are not made to be two "individualists" but a team working together. This unity of "one flesh" is intended to be physical (sexual), social (companionship), spiritual (communion with God) and in other ways. It is to be carried out regularly in such a way as to increase mutual joy, serve God's interests, serve others and model what God intended. Disunity and strife are not God's will in any human relationship. This can be healed through mutual submission to God's will, as revealed in the Holy Scriptures. Lack of harmony has its origin (in virtually every instance) in disobedience to God.

The secular world does not accept, but defies, God's order in many ways. Some human "authorities" promote such ideas as the denying of distinction between the sexes, other than those that are biological. They promote "egalitarian marriage," meaning equality in roles, thus denying the husband's assigned role as leader, among other things. They justify marital infidelity (adultery). They may encourage living for the purpose of promoting self-fulfillment. God is sometimes presented as being androgynous, meaning to have the characteristics of both male and female. Thus He may be referred to as "she" if desired, despite Biblical references to the contrary.

We do not believe a marriage can be truly successful in all dimensions without the Lord as an essential part, acknowledging His Word as authoritative. This means that *Biblical priorities* should be observed:

1. God and His Kingdom should be first (Matt. 6:33) if you want His blessings.

2. The eternal should take precedence over the temporal (the present time) (2 Cor. 4:18).

3. The spiritual should take precedence over the physical (Matt. 6:19-20).

4. People should take precedence over things (the material) (Mark 8:36-37).

We are vainly using our few precious years when we spend our lives in such things as pursuing material accumulations, abusing television use in place of family time together, continuing all-consuming work responsibilities, leaving inadequate time for the home or the Lord and in pursuing of pleasure as the source of happiness (called hedonism).

Marriage can be one of God's greatest blessings if we learn how to live together in harmony according to the will of God. Otherwise it can be a burden, a constant source of friction, even a curse. We may have begun marriage by choosing a partner unwisely. This is often the case. Still, the Lord is rightfully called "the God of Recovery." He can turn our mistakes into something that works. He can give us "beauty for ashes" (Isa. 61:3).

One Flesh or Two Individuals?

DISCUSSION QUESTIONS

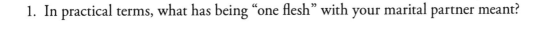

1. In practical terms, what has being "one flesh" with your marital partner meant?

2. Can you list at least two areas in which you tend to think and act individualistically where you should be more of a team player?

3. What are the priorities in your marriage relationship? To what extent are you both agreed in this area?

4. What has been the greatest blessing (or blessings) that you have enjoyed in marriage?

5. What has been the greatest challenge (or challenges) that you encountered in marriage? How have you dealt with them??

Understanding GENUINE *Love* IN *Marriage*

Love has always been a major topic for popular stories, motion pictures, songs and everyday conversation. However, understanding exactly how to define or practice love seems to have eluded most people. It is considered to be the most important quality in a lasting marriage. This is so in any close relationship. Love seems to be the major deficient element in troubled marriages. A writer once said, "The course of true love never did run smooth." If this is so, what advice can be given to repair relationships that can in no way be characterized by true love?

Is love a romantic feeling? Is it simply another word for sexual intercourse? Should it be geared to meet whatever demands or desires are imposed by others? ("If you loved me, you would do it.") Is its primary object self-gratification? Does love mean the same thing in every usage? Do we love God, love our family members, love certain experiences and even love certain foods in the same way because we use the same word? In particular, what is the meaning in Ephesians 5:25 when it says, "Husbands love your wives"?

In the Greek language of the New Testament, different words were used to express differing concepts. In English and other languages, we tend to use the same word (love) for all. *Eros*, from which we get our word erotic, means physical love. *Phileo*, from which the city of Philadelphia is named, means brotherly love. *Agape* means sacrificial or self-giving love. We have no comparative term. The greatest passage in Scripture on the subject of agape love is 1 Corinthians 13, especially verses 4–5. There it is described as patient and kind. It is not jealous, not arrogant, not self-serving, not easily provoked and not willing to retain grievances. The description of what love is *not* is instructive.

Love is used most often in Scripture as a verb, meaning it is something you do, rather than something you *feel*. We are commanded by the Lord to love our enemies (Matt. 5:44), which surely is not based on feelings. The command is addressed to the will of man, not to his emotions. It has been objected that a person cannot show love to others if they have never experienced love. Is this the only way we can learn about it? Can we grow out of immaturity, selfishness and the handicap of an unloving background by responding to Christ's love for us? Can we learn from His example, be motivated by His love and respond because of it to His command to us in His enabling power? Is this too hard for God to do in a yielded vessel? There is a clear command in Scripture to love God. It is called "the first and the greatest commandment." The second is to love others. There is no command to love self. Being a lover of self is to join with a group of unholy practices such as are named in 2 Timothy 3:2–4. The self-sacrificial character of true love is seen in Ephesians 5:25: "Christ loved the church and *gave Himself up* for her." This kind of love is the model for the husband's love for his wife. A wife's love for her husband is indicated by showing respect (Eph. 5:33) and submission to his leadership (Eph. 5:24). Husbands and wives may not *feel* like doing any of this. However, they can obey the lord in this matter and trust His wisdom more than any explanations or reasoning.

Men and women seem to differ in their interpretation of love in marriage. This may be based in part on differences in their nature or disposition. Husbands tend to recognize as love such efforts to please them as cooking meals they like, keeping an orderly house, maintaining a neat appearance, refraining from arguments (nagging) and cooperation. In a special way, husbands want a wife's encouragement. Wives on their part want to be shown affection (not necessarily sex), be appreciated, not "taken for granted" or seen as simply useful around the house. Some Japanese men have an interesting, if disturbing, word they use for their wives; it is translated "the thing in the house." An American wife would hate being regarded in this manner.

A loving wife will check her tendencies to criticize or belittle her husband, especially before others. She will not see him simply as someone who brings home the paycheck or helps around the house. A loving husband will check his tendencies to be overly critical, harsh or indifferent. This is often shown by ignoring her unless he wants sex. A good husband will be considerate of his wife's tender sensitivities. He will remember that she may have more interest than he does in keeping alive some degree of the romance that once characterized their relationship. He will look for opportunities to compliment her in a thoughtful way, or be considerate when she is weary or troubled. Tenderness is greatly desired by most women from their husbands. She wants to be cherished (held dear), not regarded as chattel (something you possess). Abuse of a woman, verbally but especially physically, is intolerable. There is no excuse for it.

It may be helpful for both partners to sit down quietly and thoughtfully to discuss issues presented above. In fact, most wives long for their husbands to talk more with them, especially about personal things. The discussion on "how to deepen our love for each other" might start with some agreement about what love is. Then each of them should list the ways in which (1) love can be shown toward my partner and (2) love can be shown to me. List some *hindrances* that ought to be removed. For example, "we never take time to talk to each other"; or, "you always jump on me when I walk through the door at night and unload on me." Be sure you are agreed *in advance* that you will not use this discussion as an occasion to start a new series of arguments and excuse-making. Just be quiet and listen thoughtfully, even if you have trouble agreeing.

Consider the following checkpoints:

1. Is your love primarily directed to benefit the other person in a constructive way, or is it selfish, just to benefit yourself?

2. Does your love clearly show evidence of personal sacrifice? We are not talking just about money.

3. Are you committed to work daily at improving the expression of love toward your partner or will you just talk and forget it?

4. Are you willing to put aside the rehashing of things that cannot be undone now? Can you forgive in your heart and now go on together for a better day?

In summary, the call to love one another in marriage, in the noblest and highest way, requires the enabling power of God. It comes to those who are yielded to His will and want to please Him. You must be motivated by the sacrificial love of Jesus for you. Otherwise, it may be beyond your effort.

Understanding Genuine Love in Marriage

DISCUSSION
QUESTIONS

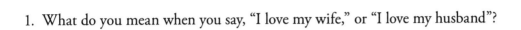

1. What do you mean when you say, "I love my wife," or "I love my husband"?

2. How do you want to be shown love in your marriage? How is it best expressed to you? *Now* say how *you* express love, or try to, to your partner.

3. Answer the four questions listed under "checkpoints" in your lesson, in the numerical order presented.

Overcoming Selfishness in the Marriage RELATIONSHIP

Perhaps the core problem of mankind, from infancy to adulthood, is selfishness or self-centeredness. It seems to be at the heart of sin. It hinders fellowship with God. It is destructive in relationships with others. It is poison in marriage. We have to battle daily in the home, if we are conscientious, with this obvious tendency in our children. It has been said that the second word a child learns after "no" is "mine." The first sentence they learn is, "That's mine." Sharing is something you have to learn; it is not innate. It doesn't help to encourage children not to be selfish when they see the example of this tendency in their parents. If we do not deal with this monster in a determined way, by God's necessary enablement, it will continue to undermine essential harmony within marriage.

Self-centered thinking inevitably produces friction and then open clashes. Perhaps we call it lack of consideration, thoughtlessness or insensitivity, which are milder descriptions of the problem of the self life. Statements such as "I want," "I think," or "I feel" are common. These are seldom turned around to ask what the other person wants, thinks or feels. How things affect *me* is what concerns the self-centered person. But how does this seem to the Lord? How is this affecting our children? Does it matter enough to exercise self-restraint or to put my own interests in a secondary position?

The Lord Jesus dealt with this "me first" attitude often in His earthly ministry. It was very evident in disputes among the disciples who debated among themselves who should be the greatest in the coming kingdom (Mark 9:33-34). He rebuked them by teaching that if they wanted to be the greatest, they should first learn to be the servant of all and take the lowest position. The Lord taught that pleasing God should come first in our lives. Loving and serving others came next. In His own example, He suffered and died for others. He did not come to have others serve Him but to serve *them* (Matt. 20:28). He said, "If anyone wishes to come after me, let him deny himself and take up his cross and follow me" (Matt. 16:24). In Philippians 2:3-4 we read, "Do nothing from selfish ambition or empty conceit, but with humility of mind let each of you regard one another as *more important than himself.* Do not merely look out for your own interests, but also for the interests of others."

None of this emphasis is evident in current secular recommendations about dealing with marriage problems. Instead, we hear about demanding your "rights," standing up for yourself or asserting yourself. The standard advice is "Don't put up with it!" With this kind of counsel, no wonder we have the highest divorce rate in the world, with families disintegrating on every hand. People do not want to deal with themselves. They want to get rid of circumstances by any means.

How can any of us deal successfully with selfishness in our marriages? It's not easy. In our fleshly strength doubtless we will not succeed. It will take supernatural enablement to overcome this sinful tendency inherent in our natures. Selfishness comes naturally. In the course of life this tendency may have been softened, modified and trained to a more acceptable way of expressing itself. However, the root remains. The first step to overcoming this is to be born again and indwelt by the Holy Spirit to empower transformation. There is then a resident power from above to deal with this. This alone is not enough. Unless we as believers daily yield ourselves to the Spirit's *control*, we will lapse into our natural, selfish ways.

Carefully consider some of these guidelines for an anti-selfishness program in your marriage:

1. Commit yourself daily to live, speak and relate to your partner under the Lordship of Christ. Resolve to let Jesus be your guide, not your emotions.

2. Do a fearless daily inventory of your actions and speech, perhaps before retiring at night. It is a great time to review the day and make necessary confessions. Were you self-centered and insensitive to your mate at any point? Swallow your pride and confess it, first to God, then to your marriage partner. It is helpful to admit frankly, "I was wrong," without excuses.

3. Have a periodic review session with your mate (weekly at first) and invite one another to point out what appeared to be selfish, insensitive or manipulative. Do not argue when you get bad news. Don't make excuses or look disgusted. Just listen and think about what you are hearing. Don't plead, "Nobody is perfect. I'm only human."

4. *Where* specifically have you put yourself to some trouble or inconvenience to serve the other person's interests? List the positive acts intended by you to show a sacrificial spirit toward your partner. Refraining from negative actions is good. Trying consistently to be kind and thoughtful is even better. Are you seeking to look out for your partner's needs, or mainly involved with thinking about your own needs?

5. Could you be perceived as frequently (or occasionally) insisting on your own way? Ask your partner.

6. Are you taking time to listen to one another regularly? Maybe you are just too busy or too bored to make the effort. "He never listens to me" is a very common phrase heard in many households.

7. Is a good relationship with your partner a *priority* in your thinking? It may be that the person is difficult to live with, at times, or drains your supply of patience. If so, pause for a moment and consider how patient the Lord Jesus has been with you.

Now, after thinking carefully about these issues and questions, talk about them, one by one, with your partner. Be thoughtful. Be a *good* listener. Then write down what you learned in one of the discussion questions covering these issues.

Overcoming Selfishness in the Marriage Relationship

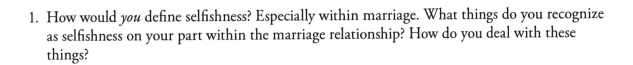

DISCUSSION
QUESTIONS

1. How would *you* define selfishness? Especially within marriage. What things do you recognize as selfishness on your part within the marriage relationship? How do you deal with these things?

2. Review the guidelines given in the lesson. Check the ones that you can agree are problems within the relationship, whether on the husband's part or the wife's part. What needs to be done? Are you committed to begin action?

3. Layout the beginning of your plan to deal with these things with a view to at least *limit* them, if not remove them from your life.

IMPROVING Communication *in* Marriage

A recently released study, done by the Gallup Public Opinion Poll, makes this statement: "A couple's ability to communicate is the single most important contributing factor to a stable and satisfying relationship. The quality of relationships among couples with excellent communication is strikingly better than those with less satisfactory communication."

It is possible that other factors in the marriage *contribute* to unsatisfactory communication. They might include major unresolved differences, financial pressures, spiritual problems, unfaithfulness, alcohol abuse, TV overuse or just lack of knowledge on how to communicate. It is something that needs to be addressed. There must be a desire by both parties to overcome any hindrances and to develop necessary skills. Significantly, Gallup said that the level of *trust* in a relationship appears closely tied to the couple's ability to communicate.

What is real communication? It has been defined as *something* that *takes place* when there is a meeting of meanings between two or more persons. In other words, this is more than someone "saying your piece," or "getting something off your chest." Henry Brandt, a Christian counselor, says "to communicate means to overcome the desire to conceal feelings and thoughts which lead to honesty of expression." This is more than dialogue merely consisting of words and responses between persons.

In Scripture, no single word fully expresses what is meant by communication. Two words that are close are, *Koinonia* (Heb. 13:16; 1 Tim. 6:18), which means participation, partnership and fellowship and *Homileo* (Luke 24:15) which means to be in company with or converse. Supremely, the Lord Jesus *is* the Word, the communication of God to man. In God's creation, articulate speech and writing are His gift to man, distinguishing him from all other creatures.

It has been said that understanding involves more than talking in effective communication. Otherwise, an exchange of words may degenerate into a "dialogue of the deaf." This means that neither partner really listens to the other. From one's own viewpoint, it should be more important to *understand the other person* than for the other person to understand me. This is where unselfishness needs to be evident if you want effective communication within marriage. Good communication is not simply the passing along of acts or a reporting of incidents, although they may have their place. The understanding of the other person's inner attitudes and thinking is important. We ought to *care* about this, not just establish our own opinion.

George Sanchez of the Navigators has written and taught extensively about marriage, including communication. He has emphasized the need for what he calls *disciplined listening*, a very helpful expression. He recommends the following:

1. ***Listen for emotional overtones.***
   When there is evidence of hurt, anger, bitterness, frustration and discouragement, we ought to pick it up immediately. This in itself is most important to explore and resolve.

2. ***Ask questions to clarify.***
   Don't jump to conclusions. Are you sure you understand the facts or issues? You should compliment a person and give encouragement. You evidence the fact that you sincerely *want* to understand.

3. ***Avoid defensive reactions.***
   This means to quickly take offense at what is said so that you begin to justify your words or actions. Some of this *may* come from pride. Is it too much for you to have someone criticize you or disagree? There may be something we can learn from our critics, however small. They may tell us something we need to think about. Pause and think things over before replying. Begin with a phrase like, "You may be right."

4. ***Don't tune out.***
   Don't stop listening if the pattern or issue sounds familiar ("I've heard all this before"). It may be "the same old stuff" to you, but let's confer on how to resolve or deal with something if it's that important to *them*.

5. ***Don't listen only to what interests you.***
   This is called selective listening. The idea in communication is two-way participation and understanding. This is not a solo game. What interests the other person is important to *them*.

6. ***Don't let your mind wander.***
   It is easy to have your eyes "glaze over" or your thoughts sidetracked during an exchange. Call it preoccupation with something else or even worry. Remember however that it is usually noticed. It says, "I'm not interested in what you are saying."

7. ***Don't let trigger words turn you off.***
   Certain expressions (or subjects) may have some unusual way of causing you to erupt. Restrain your emotions. Remember too that certain words may "set off" your partner. Let's agree on what they are. Avoid them, if possible, or find out why they are so inflammatory.

Let us add one or two more items of do's and don'ts for better conversation:

Avoid sarcasm like the plague. These are words uttered for the purpose of making a "dig" at someone, often called "needling." The last thing you should want to do is hurt someone. Words can cut deeply. It may be as simple as, "Oh sure, you're always right," with a sharp edge that means "you know it is not true." The cousin to this is what is called "kidding" or "teasing." This can easily degenerate into hurtful sarcasm. Guard against tactless, insensitive remarks.

Guard your remarks if you have a tendency to talk too long without stopping. Give the other person a chance to enter the conversation. Think of your exchange as a balloon being gently tapped back and forth between you. Do not ramble, give excessive details or repeat.

Speak up more and participate if you tend to be verbally quiet and answer with very few words. Don't let the exchange be a monologue. Don't be one who has nothing to contribute, just sitting and listening.

Ask courteous questions that show an interest. This does not mean that you act like one who is gathering information for a report. Use this formula: *Ask* a question. *Listen* to the answer. Make a *comment* on what you hear (a step often ignored), then ask again.

Concentrate on ideas, rather than upon things, personalities and unimportant details. Try to raise the level of conversation.

Do not interrupt or speak too quickly before fully hearing a matter. "He who gives an answer before he hears, it is folly and shame to him" (Prov. 18:13). Don't try to help the other person complete a sentence or otherwise cut them off. Be patient.

Learn how to discuss rather than argue. A discussion takes place when there is an exchange of views that help mutual understanding. An argument is underway when you become insistent on convincing the other person that you are right and he or she is wrong.

In conclusion, let's be committed to analyzing the hindrances to good conversation between marriage partners or even with other people. Let's study the positive principles that make conversation what it is intended to be, an essential part of real companionship. That's one of the major benefits, if not the chief one, of marriage in the first place.

Improving Communication in Marriage

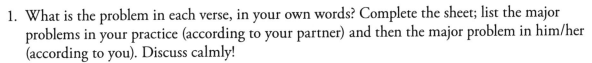

DISCUSSION
QUESTIONS

1. What is the problem in each verse, in your own words? Complete the sheet; list the major problems in your practice (according to your partner) and then the major problem in him/her (according to you). Discuss calmly!

    Part A

    Proverbs 11:12

    Proverbs 12:15

    Proverbs 12:16

    Proverbs 12:18

    Proverbs 18:2

    Proverbs 18:13

    Proverbs 21:19

    Ephesians 4:2

    Ephesians 4:26

    Ephesians 4:29

    Ephesians 4:32

    Part B

    Examine Ephesians 4:15. Answer these Questions (True or False)

    a. It does not matter what you say as long as it is loving.

    b. How you say something is very important.

    c. Being completely honest is not necessary.

    d. Truth can be spoken without harshness or tactlessness.

2. Communication check list: each partner should make a check to the left of the problem they experience (not the other person). Then sit down and review your answers and see if you can agree. Accept the other person's evaluation of you. Circle five or six problems concerning yourself and seek to improve in these areas.

    Deficiencies in Effective Listening

    My nonverbal mannerisms (bored, disgusted looks)

    My prior feelings or grievances

    My interruptions (as they perceive it)

    My tendencies to talk too long (not "coming up for air")

    My lack of interest in the subject

    My feeling that I know the subject better

    My feeling that often I don't understand what he/she is saying

My lack of concentration

My misunderstanding of their point of view

My failure to clarify matters

My feeling that they talked too long

My own bias on certain subjects

My unwillingness to let my partner share his/her real feelings

My tendency to be over-critical

My lack of confiding in them

Deficiencies in Responding

My use of sarcasm or "put downs" (as they see it)

My tendency to react emotionally, impulsively

My fear of receiving a negative reaction

My weakness in seeing my partner's point of view

My failure to give verbal feedback

My failure to notice their feedback to me

My lack of knowing exactly what to say

My lack of warmth and empathy

My lack of clear understandable comments

My lack of any real, direct response

My inability to allow others to disagree with me

General Barriers to All Communication

Difficulty in distinguishing fact from opinion

Poor timing (when is this generally?)

Fatigue, too worn out (is there a better time?)

Feelings of being pressured, overpowered (how to backoff)

Situation gets too emotional (what then?)

Frustration, desire to quit trying (what can be done to resolve this?)

Not making the effort needed (what will it take?)

Do not feel free to be honest (same as above—fear of reaction, revealing a possible fear or weakness, etc.)

Our exchanges are often monologues (why?)

I think there is no use (why?) — List any others not mentioned

THREE *Principles for Getting Along*

There have been many principles suggested by various "experts" about how to get along with one another. You could list 100 do's and don'ts. You probably could not remember to practice most of them if they were listed. Hopefully we can present three major suggestions. They might make a big difference in how you can have a better relationship with your partner, even if only one of the mates makes a serious effort. Of course, it's ideal if both of you make the effort. In other words, will you try?

The three major principles are:

1. ***Accept personal responsibility*** for all of your own actions, attitudes, words and other responses. Do not be a "blame-shifter."

2. ***Forget the past,*** rather than continue bringing up old grievances or complaints that you thought had been settled, forgiven, and forgotten (Phil. 3:13b; Mark 11:25—26). When can you make a fresh start and forget what lies behind?

3. ***Commit yourself to helping one another in character development.*** Are you working to stimulate one another to love and good works? (Heb. 10:24). Growing in this area is one of the most important opportunities in a marriage relationship. Are you working on it?

You might consider each of these principles in the order presented, since one can lead to those that follow. This supposes that you are making a thoughtful effort to develop a better marriage. Identifying areas for improvement is a preliminary, but necessary, step to the larger task. This is to go to work on the problem in a *serious way*. You need to be marital *house cleaners* of negative factors and *house-builders* in a positive way. We refer to the house of your marriage relationship.

1. Accepting personal responsibility.

It seems difficult for people to avoid making excuses or blaming others for something they have said, done or failed to do, particularly if the outcome is not good. Blame-shifting seems to have been the first action of our parents in the Garden of Eden (Gen. 3:8-15) when confronted by God about their sin. It seems clear in Scripture that God is not going to allow excuse-making to prevent any disciplinary action on His part. He certainly did not accept the excuses of Adam and Eve. Neither will He accept our attempt to escape responsibility for our behavior.

Blame-shifting for disobedience or poor behavior is a typical activity of children. It seems to be natural to them. "He started it" or "I didn't hear you," are but two typical excuses in childishness. It takes maturity and character to honestly admit our own responsibility and say, "I was wrong."

When it is said of someone, "he never admits he is wrong," we are talking about weak character and hypocrisy. One of the major principles of most contemporary psychiatry and psychology is that of sanctioning excuse-making and blame-shifting. Everything and everyone, past or present, societal or individual, is a target for blame and is an attempt to escape personal responsibility. Someone takes the place of being a "victim" and counselors usually sympathetically lend support.

Within marriage it is absolutely frustrating to try to resolve problems with a partner who finds it almost impossible to accept responsibility for whatever action taken or words said. Whatever the supposed provocation or situation, we alone are responsible for our responses. God will hold us to that even if others do not. Some have a habit of admitting wrong in a small way, then following with the word "but." Others should pay attention only to what comes after the "but." That is why someone once said, "But me no 'buts.'"

Agree between yourselves on these two practices:

➢ No matter why I said or did something I am still accountable to God, and others who may be involved, for my responses. Misbehavior or irresponsibility on the part of others cannot be used properly to excuse a wrong response on my part.

➢ Partial admission by me of responding wrongly, especially when followed by "but," does *not* constitute accepting personal responsibility. *Whatever* you or others did, your response was either right or wrong in God's sight. Admit it and offer no excuses. That evidences strength of character, not weakness.

2. Forgetting the past.

Some philosopher once said, "To err is human but to forgive is divine." This means that all human beings have done or said something that is wrong and regrettable in their past. The same human beings find it hard to forgive and forget the wrongs they have suffered from others in the past. Yet they look to God to forgive them for their own sins. It is on this basis that we are commanded in Ephesians 4:32, "Be kind to one another, tender-hearted, forgiving each other, just as God in Christ also forgave you." God forgave us in grace, not because we deserved His forgiveness. He expects us to act toward others in the same way—certainly to our marriage partners.

This does not mean that we overlook persistent, unrepentant misconduct. It means that once made right by confession, forsaking of sin and true repentance, we ought to do what God does, put it behind us and be done with it. When you have done all you can now to make things right with your partner, that is all you can do. For the other person to keep bringing it up and "throwing it in your face" repeatedly, long afterward, is a despising of God's own graciousness to us. The Lord Jesus solemnly warned His listeners of the sin of this behavior in Matthew 18:23–35. He called the unforgiving person "wicked" and said God would treat them in the same manner they treated others.

Marriage partners often do not move promptly to settle grievances. Ephesians 4:26 says, "Do not allow the sun to go down on your anger." This means, do not carry over any grievances against your partner to the next day. They tend to grow worse as both parties brood over the incident. It is a part of our sinful nature to nurse (hold tightly) our grievances against others. This may be because we want to punish them somehow. It may be because we want to justify our own attitudes and actions. People often say, "I can't forget it" or "I can't forgive him or her." They really mean, "I won't." Unresolved, unforgiven grievances act like acid in the soul. They defile our relationship with God and embitter our spirits. When you come short of the grace of God in this way, then the "root of bitterness springing up causes trouble and by it many are defiled" (Heb. 12:15). It is spiritually and emotionally healthy to put the past behind you.

3. Helping one another in character development.

It is impossible to rightly understand the dealings of God with His children in the circumstances of life without seeing His work in character development. This is summarized as the goal of conforming us to the moral likeness of His Son (Rom. 8:24; 2 Cor. 3:18). God is working to restore His image in us (Gen. 1:27). This image has been marred by sin and needs restoration (1 Cor. 15:49).

Since marriage is divinely instituted, then one of its purposes must be to perfect our characters through marital interaction. If we are to grow in our marriages we must grow in our characters. Therefore, those partners who are genuine believers must dedicate themselves to this. First, we should seek to grow ourselves in handling various aspects of the union. Second, we should consider how we can help our mates grow and not be a hindrance to them. This may be a new thought to many couples. However, if it is made a part of our thinking, it can be a positive contributing factor to improvement. Admittedly, this viewpoint will require a great deal of maturity.

God has commanded us to grow in all aspects (Eph. 4: 15).

Growth means change. Character growth is a gradual process, not an overnight venture. It requires the yieldedness of the believer to God's spiritual control. It also requires our cooperation with others. This involves the willingness to listen and to be open to change.

We can be *hindered in growth* in many ways. Most of us tend to resist personal change, whether due to complacency, pride, stubbornness, insensitivity or lack of belief that it is possible. We may resent being reminded or corrected by others, perhaps in a special way by our marriage partner. If we are not open to change, then it will not happen. Our lives and our marriages will suffer accordingly. *We* lose.

How can we help one another, without becoming "naggers," or carping critics? Hebrews 10:24 says, "Let us consider how to stimulate one another to love and good deeds." How can we assist one another in a proper way? The first need is to be an *example*, especially in the area in which we want others to change. Remember, the goal is Christ-likeness, not what you would like personally.

What other things can we do to help? We can *pray* for them in specific areas in a believing way. We can learn how to use honest praise and encouragement for even small steps of progress. *Encouragement* is a great motivator. There is both a positive and a negative way to make suggestions. Learn the difference. Discover how to put forth a suggestion in a constructive, affirmative way. Can you have times of honest dialogue, in a spirit of meekness, without someone erupting emotionally? You ought to discover how to do this successfully. Establish some ground rules. If you can give it out, can you also "take it"? Define by discussion and example what you are talking about! Get into the Word together; pray together about your differences. Seek to be tolerant of emotional and personality differences. Think in terms of the other person's benefit. Study the attributes of God. Many of them can be established as areas for your own improvement.

In summary, commit yourself as a couple to developing the kind of maturity which will enable you to deal with the issues presented in this lesson. Yield yourselves and your marriage to the Holy Spirit so He can empower you to succeed where otherwise you will fail. "With God *all* things are possible," said the Lord Jesus.

Three Principles for Getting Along

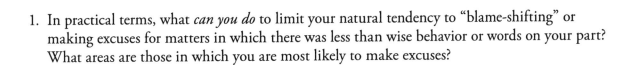

DISCUSSION
QUESTIONS

1. In practical terms, what *can you do* to limit your natural tendency to "blame-shifting" or making excuses for matters in which there was less than wise behavior or words on your part? What areas are those in which you are most likely to make excuses?

2. How do you handle the matter of grievances or offenses by your partner that are a part of the past? When and why do you bring them up during current disputes? What could you do to eliminate this habit?

3. List the ways in which you could contribute to your partner's character growth in a constructive way. Do not just list what was in the lesson; put down what you are willing and able to do.

4. Of the three principles listed in this lesson, with supporting details, what made the most impact on your thinking? Do you believe this can be a positive influence on having a better marriage?

REDUCING *Arguments* and *Misunderstandings*

There will always be differences between human beings, sometimes leading to disagreements; but must we be disagreeable? This means unpleasant, argumentative, discourteous and bad-mannered. To this can be added being angry, caustic, cutting, irritating and offensive in tone, manner or word. Not one of these characteristics is helpful in resolving, as followers of Jesus, an otherwise legitimate difference of opinion.

James 4:1 asks, "What is the source of quarrels and conflicts among you? Is it not the source of your pleasures (*desires*) that wage war among your members?" The source then is not the area of disagreement, or the other person, but within our own sinful natures. We wish to be proven right. The other person must be proven wrong. We lust to have "the last word." We wish to win the argument, at any price. Now what would you call this attitude? A change in it by God's enabling power could be the point of beginning in reducing arguments. It would improve our ability to behave *like Christians* when we have differences.

Argumentative people, professing to be followers of Christ, seem to have forgotten Galatians 5:19-20: "Now the deeds of the flesh are evident, which are: strife, jealousy, outbursts of anger, disputes, and dissensions." These sins are set in contrast to the fruit of the Spirit in verse 22. The practice of evil deeds of the flesh calls into question the reality of whether we are truly Christians who are heaven-bound (v. 21). That is a very serious matter. The issue therefore is whether *our own behavior* is in accordance with the faith we profess. Our partners may be difficult, or at least we think they are. This really doesn't change our accountability to God to respond properly in provocative situations. Remember, we are not permitted, in God's sight, to excuse wrong behavior on our part by blaming someone else!

This does not mean that we are to be without convictions, or even opinions. We certainly need to learn how to express our opinions to our partners, without the discussion degenerating into an argument and consequent ill will. There is a difference between a discussion and an argument, and we must learn to agree on the difference. We *discuss* something when both parties have an opportunity to present certain matters for the other's consideration. Discussions are not monologues; they are *not* an attempt to win an admission that we are right and they are wrong. They are *not* angry exchanges which bring heat but very little light. In discussion, people listen with respect (not necessarily agreement) to the other person's point of view, however mistaken it may be.

When a discussion turns to an argument, it ought to be terminated because it serves no useful purpose; It is harmful. When children hear their parents having an argument, or even evidencing tenseness in their relationship, it is extremely harmful to them and a poor example. They may see "life as it is," as some defenders claim. They certainly do not see life as it ought to be. Other words for this are *quarrels* (verbal conflict of complaints or prolonged, often noisy disputes) and *bickering* (impatient and irritable exchanges which continue). The most common domestic term is *fight*, sometimes called a "row," "blow-up" or "explosion." In extreme situations a person is said to "rant and rave."

The distress of all this is expressed in Proverbs 21:9 where it is said that it is "better to live in a corner of a roof than in a house shared with a contentious person." Proverbs 17:14 says that at the very beginning of strife, it ought to be terminated, for the good of all. A prominent Christian once told the author that he and his wife never argue. When I asked the reason for this remarkable achievement, he said, "My wife refuses to argue." This seems almost too much to expect, however, for most marriage partners. How then do we reduce arguments and misunderstandings?

1. ***Try to control your responses.*** Allow the Lord, in fact beg Him, to control your emotions, words and actions. Self-control is one of the fruits of the Spirit, or Spirit-controlled life. This comes from a daily interaction with God. We ought then to practice Romans 6:6, 11, 13 and 8:13. They say we should know, reckon, yield and "put to death" certain things. This leads to an overcoming life. Proverbs 25:28 says that a man who has no control over his (own) spirit is like a city that is broken into and without walls. Proverbs 15:1 says, "A gentle answer turns away wrath, but a harsh word stirs up anger." Proverbs 29:11 says, "A fool always loses his temper but a wise man holds it back." Angry people stir up strife which leads to sin. (Prov. 29:22). This is linked with pride in the following verses. In summary, cool off and hold your fire before speaking hostilely and angrily. Learn to *listen* better and "spout off" less.

2. ***Learn to overlook offenses,*** real or imagined. Understand and practice forbearance (Eph. 4:2; Col. 3:13). This means to "put up with," or endure. It is for Christ's sake and the common good. Proverbs 19:11 says it is the glory of man to "overlook a transgression," the outcome of a willingness to restrain anger. Remember the attitude of the Lord Jesus before Pontius Pilate or the accusers. Consider His restraint and grace. A forbearing person could, perhaps even justly, say something, but declines to do so. He holds his peace, exhibiting patience, humility and gentleness. This is a display of very strong character. It is Christ-like. Determine to overlook things rather than be offended, as a daily practice, especially in the home.

3. ***Where differences are quite real and cannot be overlooked,*** try to resolve them in a reasonable way. Select a good time to work on issues. Avoid times when you are tired, hungry, angry or highly emotional. Agree to speak calmly in a conversational tone (not high pitched or fast paced). Work towards resolving differences, not in

a "win-lose" atmosphere. Learn to concede failings of attitude or practice. Write down the pros and cons of issues in a way which includes both points of view and the reasons for them. Decide what is achievable in the way of agreement. Compromise points of view, without compromising convictions. Again, this takes a great deal of maturity and spiritual strength. However, it is worth your efforts to achieve this in communication, leading to settling issues peacefully.

4. ***Where you cannot seem to resolve things*** between yourselves on major issues, try to agree on a mature believer to help as an arbitrator. Agree to make his recommendation binding on the matter. This can be a formal or informal setting. The goal is to settle the matter and get it behind you. Smoldering disputes are a danger in your relationship. Break through any impasse.

Here are some unhealthy examples of speaking in trying to settle things:

➢ "It's hopeless. I have given up even trying. He (or she) will never change."

➢ "I intend to get this off my chest" and "set you straight."

➢ "I don't even want to talk about it, now or ever. I don't wish to deal with it."

To these examples you can add various accusations, denunciations and exasperation.

Ask yourself these questions:

1. Are my responses characterized by *grace* (undeserved favor), just as the Lord has dealt with me?

2. Am I willing to at least share responsibility for this conflict? Or do I put this totally on the other person?

3. Are we moving in a good direction, even though everything is not perfect? Am I expecting perfection in our relationship in a world of imperfect people?

4. Am I fully committed, even sacrificially, to eliminate things that tear down our relationship by causing disharmony?

5. Is my goal to eliminate, or minimize, quarreling in my home? If not, why not?

Learning how to handle and eliminate arguments and misunderstandings is a marriage builder and home builder in atmosphere. Make it a priority.

Reducing Arguments and Misunderstandings

DISCUSSION
QUESTIONS

1. In your opinion, *why* do you have marital arguments, especially those which lead to ill will and hurt feelings?

2. What in your opinion would reduce the frequency and negative impact of arguments and misunderstandings in your marriage?

3. If you could come to a mutually satisfactory agreement on one or more issues in which severe arguments have arisen, what would they be?

RESOLVING
Problems and
Frustrations

"**I**'m so frustrated that I don't know what to do."

What a common outcry today! What does it mean? It is a deep sense of ineffectiveness and dissatisfaction, arising from unresolved problems. We feel blocked from succeeding in situations we have tried and failed to make right. We feel like giving up, but in marriage particularly there is a high price tag for giving up.

Why do we want to give up when frustrated? We may be disappointed with the results of our own efforts. "I have done all I know to do and nothing seems to work," some say. We may be disappointed with the efforts that others make. "He never listens, never changes and never does what he should." We may be disappointed with failures in the daily experiences of life, thus affecting the marriage.

Why are we so frustrated rather than hopeful?

1. Perhaps we have not accepted the fact that imperfection is a part of life here on earth. Problems, difficulties and disappointments are normal. These are the things with which we must learn to deal. Some things need to be accepted while others can be overcome. This is a part of life.

2. Perhaps we have not consistently and persistently looked to the Lord for His supernatural power to overcome difficulties. "Is anything too difficult for me?" God asks (Jer. 32:27). Is the problem that our faith is too small, not even as a mustard seed? Is human inadequacy a barrier to the working of God?

3. Perhaps we have not learned how to see disappointments as a means of growth. Is there no place for being tested and learning important lessons in times of difficulty? We may need to learn how to handle these things without exploding in anger or lapsing into a melancholy state, or just quitting.

In a special way, what do wives often do when frustrated? They may cry, as an emotional release. They may become angry. They may become depressed. They may consider certain, damaging actions that they would ordinarily overlook.

What do husbands often do in these situations? They may become verbally or physically violent. They may become angry without being violent. They may become depressed, or go silent. They may also consider certain actions as harmful that they would ordinarily pass over. To review these actions ought to convince us that none of them are helpful. Surely, there is a more constructive way to deal with frustration.

What could we do *constructively* in place of the above?

1. *Calm down* and try to remove the emotional element from your responses.

2. *Pray and seek God's guidance* for what is best. Maybe a period of "waiting on the Lord" would be better than anything you have been doing. Spend more time in the Scriptures, not less. Open up your mind to divinely given insights.

3. *Analyze the situation* in a fresh way. Your thinking may be "in a rut." Consult a wise, mature believer for counsel. Seek a new perspective—clarify your thinking. Reduce your "ventilating" (spouting off). Don't expect a counselor to "fix" your partner. That's not a counselor's job. He or she probably couldn't do it anyway.

4. *Set up a quiet time* to review things calmly with your partner; look for ways to relieve frustration and improve the situation. This is not a time for renewing a "war of words."

5. *Consider a change in your regular routine of life.* Do something together that you enjoy, as a tension reliever. Try to get some extra rest, consider a trip to the park, to the beach or to the mountains. Get your mind out of its rut. Stop talking or thinking about your frustration for awhile. Break your cycle of thinking and be open to something fresh.

6. *Stop demanding that your partner live up to your expectations* or conform to your thinking: Perhaps your expectations are not realistic. Are you comparing your partner to someone else or a fantasy image? Did you marry with a view to change that person? Remember that *you* cannot change your partner, especially with *your* talking (nagging) and maneuvers.

   Your partner will change only when he or she is finally willing to change, not before. He or she will change when they are willing to listen to God and/or mature counsel. Only then will God's enabling power work in their lives.

7. *Learn to accept what you cannot change.* Change whatever you can properly, especially about yourself.

8. *Avoid quickly reckoning bad motives or lack of caring* to your partner. Give them credit for doing better when you can. There may be greater effort, or restraint, than you think.

9. *Deal with your own negative emotions* before correcting your partner. Correction does not go over well when you are upset, resentful or when you have been giving the other person "the silent treatment."

10. *Work for harmony rather than victory* (I'm right and you're wrong). Don't try to have "the last word."

Being frustrated is a poor way to succeed at anything. It is a negative reaction to what you don't like. It is not constructive. Remember that *your* actions and attitudes are *your* problems. You are not responsible for what the other person does or doesn't do, but for what you do. Do what is right for the Lord's sake. It will give the best results.

Remember there is a good side to problems. You can grow in character by being an overcomer with God's help. Learn to be a stronger, better person. You glorify God by overcoming problems through obedience and submission to Him. Learn to draw strength from God as the branches from the vine (John 15:10b). By learning to be a wiser person, instead of stewing in your frustrations, you grow in "the school of God." Don't ask God to give you fewer problems and frustrations— Ask Him to help you be a better person.

DISCUSSION QUESTIONS

1. What things do you need to eliminate in your own life and reactions in order to overcome frustrations with your partner?

2. Of all the constructive ways to deal with frustration listed in this lesson, which ones do you choose to put into practice in your life?

3. Discuss your answers with your partner calmly and see how you both can help each other improve in this area. List the agreements or plan of action.

Understanding AREAS OF Sexual Differences

When God created "male and female" (Gen. 1:27; 5:2), He made them different. This is not inequality but difference. This difference is more than a matter of biological or physical distinction. It involves personality and real gender differences. This includes the way we respond emotionally, the way we reason, and the decisions we make. It involves our appointed roles in the home and in the church. It also affects the way we respond sexually.

If we fail to understand these differences in temperament and sexual response, we can cause misunderstanding, dissatisfaction and frustration in the marriage relationship. The common but erroneous mind-set of marriage partners is that the partner could or should respond just as we do. This is a fundamental mistake. Consider the following brief reminders:

1. Men are usually quick in sexual responses. Women require a longer period of arousal.

2. Men are stimulated visually while women respond more to emotional factors.

3. Men can be aroused sexually without any personal feeling for a female—this is abnormal and often incomprehensible to a woman.

4. Atmosphere, odor, sounds, surroundings and preliminary conversation usually are not important to most men. These things mean a great deal to a woman.

5. Men are less complicated and are more highly focused in areas of sexual response. Women are sensitive in more areas.

6. When you have sexual relations, timing is much more important to a woman than to a man.

Ministering to the sexual needs of our marriage partners involves different considerations. *First*, for the believer who accepts God's Word as authoritative, there are Scriptural commands. We should take heed to what our all-wise Lord teaches us. *Second*, we should lovingly seek to understand both the biological and personality distinctions of our partner and act accordingly. In other words, we should initiate and communicate with our partners in a spiritually intelligent manner, not demanding "rights."

The Scriptural standards are simple and to the point:

1. Meet the sexual needs of your partner. Your body's "rights" belong to the other person, not to you. (1 Cor. 7:3–4). It's not something to use as a negotiating device.

2. Sexual relations within marriage are righteous in God's sight. There is nothing dirty about it (Heb. 13:4), although our earlier, pre-marital experiences may have given us a poor attitude.

3. Individuals differ, biologically, psychologically, and experientially (1 Pet. 3:7). Therefore, we must seek to understand and adapt to one another in a *mutually cooperative* way. This often requires patience and a lot of effort.

We must continue to remind ourselves that males and females are *different* in many ways. We must understand these differences and adjust accordingly.

Why do partners sometimes fail in having a mutually satisfactory sexual relationship? What can be done to correct the factors contributing to this failure? Consider these factors, among many:

1. You must be committed to working for improvement, as with any form of communication, of which sexual relations are at least a part.

2. Sexual intercourse should not be considered as something you simply "do" and that's the end of it. This attitude reduces sexual relationships to a mechanical exercise. This separates it from the concept of genuine love and mutual self-giving. *Mutual* satisfaction, with the emphasis on the *other* person, not myself, ought to be the goal.

3. Since satisfaction of *both* partners is the goal, then we ought to discuss *calmly* (listening well) what the other person feels is lacking. How can you make this part of your relationship a plus instead of a minus? For the man to consider, ask, "What is painful or untimely or unloving or simply unsatisfactory?" For the woman to consider, ask, "Am I considering his need for sexual release, or frequency or cooperation?"

4. There may be other factors than these examples. Both parties need to consider such things as fatigue and tension in the timing of an overture. There are of course limits to continually using this as an excuse. The familiar statement, "Not tonight, dear, I have a headache" and "I'm too tired," should not become a consistent refrain. Using the sexual relationship as a negotiating or manipulating device is not Biblical or acceptable.

5. Sexual relationships may be complicated by past experiences which have been bad. Such things as molestation, abuse or even previous episodes of promiscuity may have resulted in guilt feelings. Thus, sex might be considered as "dirty." It is adultery and fornication that defiles a marriage bed, not lawful, sexual relations (Heb. 13:4-5). Sometimes there are lingering feelings that sex is unclean in itself (as some sects have taught), or that celibacy is more pure (as some have taught). These may need to be resolved through wise and patient

counseling. Do not fear to discuss, using specific terms, what God was not ashamed to create. Sexual pleasure, within marriage, is a provision of God's love and wisdom. Refuse to be discouraged by past failures about the prospects for improvement. It may take some time. Be patient. It may take much honest discussion. Set aside time to do it. It may require counseling to which you will both need to take heed. If that is the case, seek it. It will certainly require, whatever the difficulties, that you should commit yourself to obey God, as directed in 1 Corinthians 7:4-5. Do not allow your "feelings" to come between you and your obedience to the Lord. Certainly we ought not to *demand* that someone else obey God. We need to do that for ourselves.

LESSON 8

Understanding Areas of Sexual Differences

DISCUSSION
QUESTIONS

1. What has opened your eyes to new thinking in this lesson? What comments would you like to add to what has been written?

2. What difficulties in the area of the sexual relationship do you think need a better understanding?

   a. For the man (by both husband and wife)

   b. For the woman (by both husband and wife)

3. What steps are needed (plan to take them) to improve your relationship in this area?

UNDERSTANDING
the Husband's
Biblical Role

In describing Biblical standards for the roles of husband and wife, we must make a frank admission. There is no honest way to make Biblical ideas acceptable to contemporary western (especially American) modernized trends. We say trends, not consensus, because the majority of ordinary Americans are still not solidly in favor of certain trends. The same can be said about the attitudes of most worldwide cultures who do not universally accept certain modern ideas about marriage.

Over the past quarter of a century, there has been a growing movement to reject, even attack, what is called the *hierarchal/patriarchal* pattern in marriage. In simple words, this means that the man should be the head of the household. In a growing percentage of cases in this culture, families don't operate that way anyway, but the idea of male headship is still accepted by the majority. Leadership is Biblical. The *modern* idea, even among a growing number of evangelicals, is that marriages should be *egalitarian* with co-leadership and interchangeable roles. Sometimes these arguments are made on the basis of a misunderstanding of the contextual flow of Ephesians 5:23-6:7. Some say there should be *mutual submission* between husbands and wives. To apply this argument to the relationship between parents and children, which follows, would be absurd. To put it more plainly, whether in marriages or other ordered relationships, somebody needs to be in charge, responsible for final decisions over all that has been said and done.

There are other modern trends which appear to undermine the distinction in roles and responsibilities in marriage. In contrast to the Biblical period, both partners today often work at regular jobs outside the home. Financial support is a joint affair. In the Bible, being a provider was the husband's responsibility (1 Tim. 5:8). The wife's main job was to be a homemaker attending to children and domestic affairs(Tit. 2:4-5). Such an idea is absolutely scorned by the modern feminist movement. The word "husband" means "keeper," just as the term "husbandman" was used to describe someone who took care of the vineyard (John 15:1). Therefore, the husband's duty is to protect and take care of his wife, of which financial support in a dependable way is a mainstay. When these roles are reversed, or even set aside for a time, it undermines respect and leadership of the husband. More to the point, it frequently causes friction and may lead to separation. The formidable responsibility for husbands is to "love your wives, just as Christ also loved the church and gave Himself for her" (Eph. 5:25). This is an infinite standard of the highest form of love, self-sacrificing in character and example. By comparison, a wife's duty is to respect (Eph. 5:33), or be subject to (Eph. 5:22), her husband. Her duty is at least practically attainable and certainly less demanding. Of those who attack or reject the concept of submission to husbands as culturally outmoded, few would be willing to regard a husband's call to sacrificial love for his wife as no longer necessary. You certainly cannot logically reject only one side of this equation.

The husband's leadership responsibility in marriage is emphasized in the qualifications for elders (1 Tim. 3:4-5). If he cannot manage his own household well, keeping his children under control with all dignity..."how will he (be able to) take care of the church of God"? In short, if he is not an effective leader, manager and supervisor of his own household and children, he should not be trusted with a similar task of taking care of God's people in the assembly. The church's leaders should model what other husbands are to do in their homes.

Husbands are called to make serious efforts to live with their wives in an understanding way, as with a weaker vessel, since she is a woman, and grant her honor as a "fellow-heir of the grace of life" (1 Pet. 3:7). This imposes a responsibility to be thoughtful, compassionate and helpful in a special way. Her status as a "weaker vessel" does not mean that she is an inferior vessel. Ordinarily, she is weaker in physical strength and may be more emotionally fragile. For example, she may be more sensitive or cry more readily. A man who treats his wife as he would treat another man is not wise, at best, and is stupid at worst.

When a husband is an effective leader, he is not harsh, tyrannical or demanding. He consults and listens to his wife where it is appropriate and shows respect to her views. If he is a good leader, he understands the necessity of being decisive and knowing when and how to make a right response. He agrees when he can and says "no" when necessary. A husband who frequently changes his mind is a great frustration to a longsuffering wife. If he is unreliable, he is painful to bear. If he is indifferent to her, it is intolerable to her nature.

For a husband to be a good manager in his home certainly does not mean that he must be involved in every small detail of the home. He must set the principles and guidelines for the home and the children. However, he must necessarily delegate the execution of some matters to the wife, just as any good manager would. It is best to stay out of being too detailed in his supervision. This is often frustrating. In short, leave as many things as possible to her discretion in certain areas. Financial matters, budget guidelines, avoidance of installment purchases and debts must all be agreed upon.

In western cultures, particularly in America, there has been a growth in the expectation of wives about their husbands contributing more in household help. This is even more important when the wife also works outside the home. Such things as taking care of the children, helping with household duties and assisting in other ways are often expected by the wife when her husband is at home. These details must be worked out between the two partners in a reasonable way. Some wives seem to have a low energy level or become easily upset. They may never be satisfied with the help given and always expect more. Some husbands may do little or nothing to help, relaxing while she toils and struggles with the children and home. A good manager would see that there must be accommodation and agreement to bring about harmony and effective function.

A wise wife realizes that she did not marry a perfect being, but one with weaknesses and frailties that are common to man. Therefore she does not demand perfection. She must be tolerant of his weaknesses and even forgiving of his failures, just as she expects him to be towards her. Kindness and a sense of humor are great assets in this regard.

There are other qualities both partners expect of each other equally, as those suggested above. The first of these is to learn how, in increasing measure, to be "easy to live with." This means, positively, that it should be a pleasure to live alongside one another in a harmonious atmosphere. Surveys have shown that marital partners expect *honesty*, not deceit or insincerity, from one another: it is a priority.

Finally, they should be agreed on goals in life: how to plan to live in a meaningful, purposeful way, especially pleasing to their Creator and Savior. As previously covered, both partners need to work on improving communication and reducing misunderstandings.

When a man works on being a good husband, he is working on something that will make life better for himself. In fact, Ephesians 5:28 says, "He who loves his own wife loves himself." More importantly, he will please his Lord and be a blessing to his wife and children.

Understanding the Husband's Biblical Role

DISCUSSION
QUESTIONS

1. In your home, what functions and responsibilities of the husband are performed well in your estimation? Discuss the answer and come to some agreement.

2. In your opinion, what could, or should, be done in practical and realistic ways to improve the husband's function? What would assist this improvement, including attitude changes on his part or hers?

3. If you are a husband, in what areas do you plan to make a serious effort to improve? If you are a wife, in what ways can you make a serious effort to help your husband improve *without* nagging or criticizing?

UNDERSTANDING
the Wife's Biblical Role

There has been something of a revolution in the concept of a wife's proper role in marriage in the Western World, especially in the United States over the past two decades. One concept that has gained ground is called *egalitarian* (equality in marriage, meaning equal leadership as well as sharing common roles at both work and home).

Admittedly, it is true that there has been much unfair treatment of women both in and out of marriage for centuries. It is scripturally true that both are equal in Christ in value and in standing (Gal. 3:28). It is questionable, however, whether the current secular and feminist ideas about roles in marriage are the same as those taught in the New Testament.

We need to examine how women should function in the Biblically defined role of a wife. We also need to look at how it relates to a better working relationship according to our differing personalities as created by God, not molded by society's latest views.

There are several important passages in Scripture regarding the primary role of married women in the home. Titus 2:3–5 says, "Older women likewise are to be reverent [godly] in behavior, not malicious gossips, nor enslaved to much wine, teaching what is good, that they encourage [or train] the young women to love their husbands, to love their children, to be sensible, pure, workers at home, kind, being subject to their own husbands that the Word of God not be dishonored." In other words, they are to be spiritual models in good behavior, to show practical love to their husbands and children, to be workers at home as a primary field of responsibility and to be subject to their husband's leadership, rather than dominating and arguing (Prov. 21:9, 19). Strife, gossip and talking too much, often unwisely, are condemned throughout Scripture for both men and women. Proverbs 31:10–31 extols the virtues of "an excellent wife" who does her husband good all of his life. She certainly is a hardworker, and is thoughtful of the needs of others.

She can *teach* other women, as well as children—she can counsel them. She can *witness* to them, visit them and show hospitality and kindness to all. In most cultures, men are not allowed to approach women, even for spiritual reasons, outside of their own immediate families. First Peter 3:4 cites the virtue of a "meek and quiet spirit" in a woman, rather than an aggressive and outspoken spirit, as is so often seen. Such women are not admirable to most people. She is to wear modest clothing which does not call attention to herself, particularly to her body (1 Tim. 2:9-10; 1 Pet. 3:3). This does not mean she must dress in some peculiar way that would attract attention in an unfavorable way. Good taste, neatness and attractiveness are acceptable within a Biblical mandate. Good works and a good character are what is to be displayed.

Lydia was a business woman, but she was also a godly woman (Acts 16:14). Phoebe was a deaconess in the assembly at Rome, serving in the practical needs of the church (Rom. 16:1). Priscilla had a spiritual ministry with her husband as a husband and wife team (Acts 18:2, 18, 26). Phillip had seven daughters who were prophetesses, but it does not say that they prophesied in the public church meetings, actions forbidden in the Word (1 Tim. 2:11-12; 1 Cor. 14:34). Deborah led the armies of Israel, but only after she protested that this was a man's job (Barak's), not hers (Judges 4:4-9). The woman described in Proverbs 31 was certainly versatile and gifted in many ways, but still a godly woman.

There is a wide and proper ministry for women in Scripture that allows her to function according to her nature and her calling by God. No woman can effectively serve God *outside* the home until she has learned to be effective *inside* the home. The same is true of husbands. How can a woman be more effective in her home duties? In many ways:

She can be neat, orderly and a good household manager. It certainly helps if she is a good cook or learns to be a better one than when she started. She can keep her own personal appearance to a good standard so her husband need not be ashamed of her or disappointed in her. That may not be easy when she feels that she has too much to do or too many small children. Still, women in past generations lacked almost all the labor-saving devices we now have, many with bigger families, and still did well. It is true that large extended families living together (grandmothers, etc.) had more who could help.

A good wife should make her home a refuge and source of rest and encouragement to her husband. If he comes home to strife, he would rather not be there. She would probably resent this also. It is important when a husband returns home from work that this is the time to make a pleasant beginning to the evening. Hold back the demands and bad news for a while. Feed him first. A wise woman once said, "When your husband is 'grumpy,' he is usually either tired or hungry."

Here are some summarizing suggestions:

1. Review the Scriptures mentioned above, plus any others that outline the wife's primary role and calling. It might also be added that single women, widows and wives abandoned by their husbands can also function in many of these same areas. Decide that you are going to live according to God's Word, not according to current secular ideas.

2. Be convinced that your joy and well being will be greatly assisted when you conform to God's will in the Biblical way rather than make excuses for not doing this. Your joy can be independent of negative circumstances, for that is at the core of God's promised enablement. Make the Lord Jesus your source of satisfaction, not your spouse. Your spouse cannot do what only God can do, satisfy you within, or make you a "fulfilled woman."

3. If you are a wife, write down areas of weakness in your own role performance. Make being a wife of excellence your goal, not a mediocre one or even a failure. Use God's standards and claim God's enablement.

4. If you are a husband, write down areas where you can help your wife, not criticize her, to be what God wants her to be.

5. Wives, help your husband be a better man, spiritually and in other ways, but not by nagging and criticizing him. Do this first by being a better wife (1 Pet. 3:1-2). Be an example. Pray. Talk less. Listen and respond constructively to both God and your husband. You can submit to his leadership without being a "doormat."

As the Lord said, "If you do these things, you will not be disappointed."

Understanding the Wife's Biblical Role

DISCUSSION
QUESTIONS

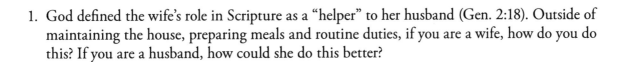

1. God defined the wife's role in Scripture as a "helper" to her husband (Gen. 2:18). Outside of maintaining the house, preparing meals and routine duties, if you are a wife, how do you do this? If you are a husband, how could she do this better?

2. In our society, it is sometimes necessary for a wife to work, yet 1 Timothy 5:14 indicates attending to the home as a primary role of the wife. How can this be worked out practically if the wife works?

3. What do you purpose to improve to make this lesson helpful in your relationship?

DEVELOPING A
Spiritual Life Together

It has been said that one of marriage's greatest blessings is companionship. This means that there will be sharing by both parties in things mutually enjoyed. Areas of sharing are social (doing things with others), *physical* (walks or other forms of exercise), and *intellectual* (sharing books, magazines, news articles). The most important area, and the most often neglected, is *spiritual*. This is the deepest level of being and the most significant for sharing.

What is spiritual sharing and what does it involve? It means that you communicate and enjoy times together in which there is direct interaction with God (prayer, reading and discussing the Word). It also includes serving together in the fellowship of His church. It means hospitality and fellowship with other believers, and witnessing or reaching out to those without Christ. The opportunity for doing these things with your marriage partner is one of the major reasons for being married to a true believer. In 2 Corinthians 6:14-15, we read, "Do not be bound together with unbelievers, for what partnership have righteousness and lawlessness or of what fellowship has light with darkness, or what has a believer in common with an unbeliever?" The answer, at the deepest level, should be "very little." Certainly they will not enjoy anything together of eternal significance. If you were not a believer, how could you "devote yourself to prayer" (1 Cor. 7:5) if your partner were not only a Christian but a serious and devoted one?

When God created two sexes and joined our first parents in marriage, He certainly intended for them to enjoy God together. He never meant for His creatures to regard fellowship with Him as only a duty, and a dull one at that. He wanted them to find satisfaction and meaning for their lives in Him. Their marriage should not hinder "undistracted devotion to the Lord" (1 Cor. 7:35). God and His interests are so great that Scripture says, "Those who have wives should be as though they had none" (1 Cor. 7:29). This does not justify neglect of primary responsibilities. It means that we are not to turn our marriages into lives absorbed chiefly with one another rather than focusing on God. Spiritual fellowship should be a major part of meaningful living as well as enjoyment. When pleasing each other becomes our major goal, rather than pleasing God, we have fallen into the trap of divided or competing interests (1 Cor. 7:33-34). God's interests then become a troublesome competitor within marriage for the time and attention of a partner. How can we have meaningful spiritual fellowship with the Lord (as a couple) and with one another?

1. You must make this a priority commitment in you lives. If you don't, it will never happen. Spiritual sharing will be "lost in the shuffle" of your business. Review by personal discussion this part of your life and determine to make any and all necessary changes. This should be the foundation of your marriage fellowship. You need to be "one flesh" in communicating with God and serving Him.

2. You both need private devotional times with God daily on your own. This can become the substance of your sharing with each other. This will enable you to speak of what the Lord has given you from the Word. It can also enable you to pray as a team on matters of mutual concern.

3. Set a time, however brief, to pray together. It is good if you can begin the day that way. Learn to get on your knees together and speak aloud to God. This can be very helpful and encouraging. Spiritually, it is a good opportunity for the husband to demonstrate leadership. If he struggles with shyness or a sense of inadequacy, make this an opportunity to grow, especially by encouragement from the wife. It is also good to pray together when there has been tension in the relationship or in dealing with difficult situations. The husband should certainly demonstrate leadership at meal times when the family is together and he gives thanks for the food.

4. The Word of God should have a central place in family life. This is more than having Bibles in the home or in a prominent location. The husband and wife should share with each other their spiritual insights. When children are present in the home, make a place for a brief family reading from the Scriptures along with applications for life. Depending on their ages, consider Bible stories (Bible storybooks are available if help is needed). Some families use interesting missionary stories. Invite appropriate participation by the children, including questions and discussions. Keep those times from being overly long or boring. Don't make it a burden.

5. Practice hospitality in your home by inviting visiting speakers or missionaries to your dinner table, or to stay with you for a short time. Many children have lifetime inspirational memories of these godly people. Bring visitors and neighbors, especially neglected persons, to your table. Think about how to live as "givers," not just "takers," in finances, time and ministry.

6. Consider how you can fellowship as a family in spiritual activities. In addition to regular church services, think of working together in special children's programs or other activities. Discuss how to improve this in family life. Both of you should serve God and contribute to the life of your church.

In summation, make the Lord Jesus and the Word of God a major part of your life together. Be more than "church-goers." There is more to Christian life than professing the name of Jesus as Lord. Let it be a living reality.

Developing a Spiritual Life Together

DISCUSSION
QUESTIONS

1. What are the greatest hindrances to spiritual sharing in your marriage and family life? What needs to be done to eliminate or reduce these hindrances? Discuss this with one another.

2. List some things you specifically plan to do to increase or improve spiritual sharing in terms of various suggestions in the lesson notes. Discuss this with one another. Be committed to what you write down.

3. Do you have any suggestions to make, based on your experience, which might help others in the class in this area?

IMPROVING
Social Time Together

One of the chief benefits of marriage is companionship. This means being together in a pleasant, harmonious and close way. When God created man and other things, He said it was "very good" (Gen. 1:31). Later He said, "It is not good for man to be alone. I will make for him a helper suitable for him" (Gen. 2:18). Man is designed, among other things, for social relationships. He is a social being, not made to live a solitary life. Chief among these social relationships is that of man and wife.

This needs to be an area of growth or development, requiring special effort. It is said in Luke 2:52 that "Jesus increased in wisdom and stature and in favor with God and man." He grew socially. The Lord, although never married, still grew in the social relationships of life. He was not a "loner," a monk or one who avoided involvement with others. He was a man of people, mingling, conversing, caring and responding to the needs of others. He appointed 12 men to be with Him for training and lived in a close personal relationship with them.

Many couples have a considerable need to work on the social aspect of their relationship. They could be together, but still lack significant, joyful social interaction. One can be married and still feel lonely because of neglect. Often, there is very little conversational exchange, even when "going out" in public. If it exists, the conversation may be so ordinary and commonplace that it is trivial and repetitive. Thus, it is dull and lacks intellectual stimulation when it could be the opposite. There could be too much talking ("she never shuts up") or too little conversation ("he never talks to me"). Perhaps the couple does not schedule regular times to "go out" together. One "killer," when there is time for social interaction, is too much television. This needs to be restricted. If you can't do that, get rid of the TV set and work on your marriage and home duties.

There needs to be real determination if improvements are going to be made. It begins with a realistic appraisal of the status of this important part of your life. If it is deficient, it ought to be acknowledged and the exact problem pinpointed. This should be followed by a plan, agreed to by both, to make whatever changes are needed. Write it out. Post it where you can see it regularly. Put your initials on it and agree that you are seriously committed to improvement.

Check the following areas where action is needed:

1. ***Good stimulating conversation on a frequent basis.*** What has prevented this? Is it that you are not committing time to it? Is it lack of "know how" or just lack of will? Is it the wrong responses, or no responses, that is killing it?

2. ***Going out with each other alone.*** When you do something enjoyable together, without distraction by children or others, you are building your social relationship. What prevents this? Is it lack of effort in setting aside regular times for this purpose? Can you agree on what you enjoy together? Or alternate between what he likes and what she likes?

3. ***Times together with friends.*** Social life should also involve other people. You can have people over to the house for a meal or refreshments. You can have a joint picnic, trip to the beach or mountains or work together on a project of mutual interest. The possibilities are numerous.

4. ***Times spent with your children or other family.*** Doing things together as a family can provide pleasant times now and good memories later, if done properly. Discuss what all of you could enjoy.

5. ***Mutually enjoyable vacations.*** Planning your vacation time can be enjoyable in itself. Do not just do what one member wants. The phrase is "mutually enjoyable." Maybe one party doesn't like "camping out" or fishing at a certain place or always going to a big commercial entertainment center. Work it out agreeably and thoughtfully.

6. ***Develop new friends or contacts.*** Reach out to your neighbors. Invite people you meet at a church gathering over for dinner. Involve yourself with other people and stay out of "ruts."

There are some limits to what you can do. An example is not enough money. You may say "all of this costs money" and "we can't afford it." This can be a problem, but it can be overcome. People in very poor communities or in poor countries often have a great tradition of hospitality. They invite one another to come and share what they have. "Potluck" meals are certainly inexpensive. This means that each person or family brings at least one dish. Public parks or other lands are usually free, or at least the fees are minimal. Have an outing at one of them. Add a picnic lunch. Set up games or activities that the group can enjoy. Many of these examples cost nothing. Be creative. Think of other possibilities. Do not allow lack of money to hinder social efforts.

Be determined to make improved social time together an important "plus" in your marriage relationship. It's a great way to make things more enjoyable, and less tense and argumentative.

Improving Social Time Together

DISCUSSION
QUESTIONS

1. List, in order of importance to you, the elements of social interaction where you feel the need of correction.

2. What have you done together socially that gave you the best memories? How often did it happen? Is it still going on or do you no longer repeat it in any form?

3. What are you planning to do now that you have studied this lesson to improve your social interaction?

Planning to Grow in YOUR Marriage

The final lesson of this series is directed to the purpose of seeing real commitment by both marriage partners to significant growth in their relationship. Without this, taking the course would be fruitless and pointless. Growth is God's desire for all living things, all spiritual life and all relationships, including marriage (Eph. 4:15). Hebrews 6:1 exhorts us, "Let us press on to maturity." The promise to those who endure trials is that by this they can become "mature and complete, lacking nothing" (Jas. 1:4). Maturity and growth are God's desire for us as individuals and as marriage partners.

A poor marriage relationship, especially when there is no evidence of improvement or little hope for such, is a poor testimony to the Lord. Others sense, despite efforts to put up a "good front," that this is less than a good relationship. If there are children, even older ones, it is damaging to them in various ways. It is required of church leaders that they have their households in order (1 Tim. 3:5). This certainly excludes those with a poor marital relationship. The situation is unacceptable to God and often miserable for the couples. To continue this way is often due to pride or stubbornness. It may be very difficult to achieve progress, especially if one of the partners does not want to make the effort. It also may not be easy to live with certain partners due to some personality quirk or other problem. Still it remains true that "with God all things are possible" (Matt. 19:26). That is why we must fervently, relentlessly seek His help. Genuine humility will bring us to be vessels of God's working. This will help us see where we may be part of the problem, not just the other person. Your goal is not to be proven right and the other person proven wrong. Our objective is to solve problems, or lessen them, so that we can have a better marriage. Therefore, a firm commitment to achieve improvement, even slowly, is essential to success.

You must consider an unhappy, tense marital relationship unacceptable to God, harmful to your children and damaging to your Christian testimony. What are you prepared to do to make improvements, starting now? Use the worksheet for this lesson to make a realistic plan.

LESSON 13

Planning to Grow in Your Marriage

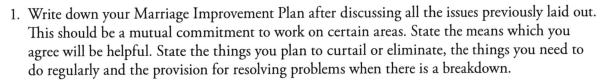

DISCUSSION
QUESTIONS

1. Write down your Marriage Improvement Plan after discussing all the issues previously laid out. This should be a mutual commitment to work on certain areas. State the means which you agree will be helpful. State the things you plan to curtail or eliminate, the things you need to do regularly and the provision for resolving problems when there is a breakdown.

   On the following checklist, mark with A, B and C the three major areas which need improvement (in order of importance or urgency):

   ___ Communication

   ___ Overcoming selfishness

   ___ Dealing with grievances

   ___ Showing love between us

   ___ Being responsible

   ___ Forgetting the past and forgiving

   ___ Following proper priorities

   ___ Role of husband, wife

   ___ Husband's leadership

   ___ Sharing spiritually

   ___ Serving others

   ___ Helping each other in character traits

   ___ Financial management and giving to God

   ___ Recreational, social time

   ___ Understanding sexual differences and needs

   ___ Handling arguments better

   ___ Resolving frustrations and disappointments

   What might be a help to you for marital growth? Check any that apply and add others:

   ___ Regular discussions (not arguments)

   ___ Seek wise counsel

   ___ Pray together for God's daily guidance

   ___ List things to be excluded or minimized (especially on my part)

   ___ Hear relevant tapes or read books

   ___ Other

2. Now list the priority areas in which you plan to work.

3. List several things you need to **stop**, need to **do**, and need to **study** (books, tapes, counseling help) under each area. List them very specifically as 1, 2, 3 and 4 under each area.

4. If you have "breakdowns" or disappointments with your partner's efforts, what will you agree to do to overcome this? Exclude nagging or a complaining spirit. Write it down.

5. Set the date and time for your first review and discussion time to monitor progress. Mark it on your calendar as you would a doctor's appointment. Allow an hour and arrange to be free of distraction or interruptions. Set the frequency of further reviews (once a month?).

6. Now write out a simple statement with both of you signing and dating it: "I am committed to make a good faith effort to improve my marriage, with God's help. Our goals, and means to reach them, are attached." Give a copy to a mature friend to whom you volunteer to make yourself accountable on a regular basis.

Notes

Notes